FOUNDERS Linda Ligon, Anne Merrow, John P. Bolton

PUBLISHER John P. Bolton

DIRECTOR OF MARKETING Haydn Strauss

EDITORIAL

EDITORIAL DIRECTOR Anne Merrow

EDITOR Linda Ligon

MANAGING EDITOR Laura Rintala

COPY EDITOR Katie Bright

CREATIVE

ART DIRECTOR Charlene Tiedemann

PRODUCTION DESIGNER Mark Dobroth

PRODUCTION MANAGER Trish Faubion

long thread
MEDIA

©Long Thread Media LLC, 2020

311 South College Avenue, Fort Collins, CO 80524; phone (888) 480-5464

ISBN 978-1-7350088-0-6 (print);
978-1-7350088-1-3 (digital)

Reproduction in whole or in part is prohibited, except by permission of the publisher.

Printed in China through Asia Pacific Offset

VISIT US ON THE WEB
www.longthreadmedia.com

I'VE BEEN THINKING ABOUT

internet, you come up with all Missouri wrapped with more t twine in Minnesota made up o of discussion forums hoping to shatter world records with the longest thread (when did that meaning enter the lexicon?). There's silkworm thread, or filament (see Michael Cook's feature beginning on page 26), which might run more than 1,500 yards in length from a single cocoon, and let's not even get into spiders.

The interesting thing to me, though, is the origin of the word. Thread. Go back a few centuries to its beginnings, and you'll see it comes from words meaning twist, or rub. In other words, a long thread is only long because you've twisted together a lot of shorter bits. I like the metaphorical implications of that. I like that the twisting or rubbing creates not just length, but strength and cohesion.

You've probably read of that ancient scrap of thread, more than forty thousand years old, spun by a Neanderthal ancestor and recently discovered in France. Not a long thread by physical measure, but incomparably long as a measure of the history of humans as thread-makers. It's thrilling to imagine: that shadowy old soul (full disclosure: I have a tad of Neanderthal DNA) sitting before a fire with a pile of carefully prepared bast fiber stripped from the inner bark of a nearby tree, twisting strands on rough stone or thigh in what we would call a counterclockwise direction, but they might call rolling against the sun. Then twisting back the other way with two other strands, twisting with the sun, to make a strong, cohesive three-ply cord. Just imagine! Eight thousand generations of thread twisting!

The utility of a long thread is beyond reckoning. Nets, traps, thongs; carrying bags, robes, blankets. Socks, T-shirts, blue jeans, high-speed internet cables . . . In this issue of *The Long Thread*, we celebrate the pleasures of discovery, creation, and connection, the hints of pure possibility inherent in our namesake. It's what we aim to be.

Linda Ligon, editor

Red Eri cocoons, page 26.

Contents

4 *Paper View*
   6   From Frogtown to Ghana with Mary Hark
  12   Aimee Lee Makes Hanji
  18   Sarah Swett and the Joy of Rubbish
  24   A flight of cranes

26 *Elegant Worm Spit*
MICHAEL COOK
A close look at silkworm cocoons
and how they come to be

42 *The Handstitched World
of Sarah K. Benning*
ANNE MERROW
A world of comfort in satin stitch

50 *Exploring Soumak*
SARA LAMB
Simple loops, but such possibilities

56 *Susanna Bauer: A Thread, A Leaf*

66 *The Wonder of Lotus Fiber*
Can it really purify your spirit?

74 *Michele Wipplinger: A Colorful Life*
KAREN SELK
Traveling rough in pursuit of natural dyes

82 *Indigo (a poem)*
SUSAN BLACKWELL RAMSEY
Blue through the ages

85 *Who Writes This Stuff Anyway?*

Core II by Susanna
Bauer, page 56.

Paper View

Chop up some wood. Your best choice would be the inner bark of certain trees, or the bast fibers of certain plants, but almost anything will do.

Boil the fragments in a caustic solution until they fall apart.

Beat them to a pulp.

Add the pulp to a water bath, then strain it into a thin layer on a screen.

Dry it flat and smooth:

Paper.

THE WAY IT IS

There's a thread you follow. It goes among
things that change. But it doesn't change.
People wonder about what you are pursuing.
You have to explain about the thread.
But it is hard for others to see.
While you hold it you can't get lost. . . .

~ WILLIAM STAFFORD

THUS HAS PAPER BEEN MADE for more than two thousand years. First in Asia, much later in Europe. Without paper, there would be no mechanically printed books. No books by and for the people. None of the 130 million or so titles published since the invention of the printing press. (If there had not been paper books, would there now be e-books?)

Making paper from shredded wood, or bark, or weeds, or rags is a story of deconstruction and regeneration. Turning paper into books is not necessarily the end of the story, though. Think of paper as raw material. Think of it as environmental stewardship. Think of it as community development.

Think of it as fun.

Mary Hark's neighbors in Saint Paul, Minnesota, pitched in and learned about papermaking with local textile refuse and biowaste.

From Frogtown to Ghana with Mary Hark

YOU CAN BEGIN WITH THE TEACHING career of Mary Hark, first as an adjunct professor at Macalester College, then as a professor at the University of Wisconsin–Madison and sought-after instructor at every major craft school in the country. Early on, she developed a specialty in papermaking, often combined with textile work; as a teacher of the craft, she has taught and nurtured hundreds.

Hark! Handmade Paper staff produced most of the 2,000-plus placemats that graced CREATE: The Community Meal.

Through the Krataa Foundation, students in Ghana learn to transform the invasive pulp mulberry, along with textile waste, into high-quality handmade paper.

But Hark's world extends far beyond academia. It's as close to home as her own Frogtown neighborhood in Saint Paul, Minnesota, and as far-flung as her papermaking workshop in Ghana, West Africa. Her world thrives on collaboration and shared visions.

CLOSE TO HOME

Look, for instance, at her involvement in CREATE: The Community Meal, a 2014 event envisioned by local artist Seitu Jones.

The goal of that project was to bring the Frogtown neighborhood together around the broad concept of sustainability and food

"*My team of papermakers not only became masterful sheet formers, but skilled and enthusiastic teachers.*"

security. This meant using locally grown and sourced food for a meal for two thousand people, with community involvement at every level. For Hark, who does not think small, it meant using the resources of her Hark! Handmade Paper Studio to produce twenty-four hundred beautiful paper place-

Inner bark stripped from invasive mulberry trees provides most of the pulp for the paper made in Hark's Ghana workshop.

mats, crafted from local textile refuse and biowaste, to grace a table a full half mile long.

"My team of papermakers not only became masterful sheet formers," she says, "but skilled and enthusiastic teachers, sharing the process with many neighbors who stopped in and tried their hands at pulling a sheet." And in the process, they helped others understand the concept of recycling and reuse at a deep level.

AND A HALF WORLD AWAY

In 1969, fourteen pulp mulberry plants (*Broussonetia papyrifera*) were brought to Ghana from China to evaluate the potential for paper production. The plan was never implemented, but the plant thrived to become a serious nonindigenous, invasive species—the very plant that has historically produced some of the world's most beautiful papers.

Forty years later, in 2009, Hark was in Ghana on a Fulbright Fellowship, captivated by the cultural and artistic richness in the textiles and, indeed, in all the country's indigenous visual arts. An invitation from the Department of Art at Kwame

Nkrumah University of Science and Technology (KNUST) in Kumasi to conduct a papermaking workshop quickly merged with a desire to make an environmental contribution by using that wonderful inner mulberry bark. The additive result would be the economic impact of training a team of producers and connecting with local markets. Once again, it's not just about the paper.

With funding from the University of Wisconsin–Madison and in collaboration with a small group of Ghana partners from the environmental, educational, business, and cultural sectors, the Krataa Foundation came to be.

Using the invasive pulp mulberry and other local botanicals, along with textile waste from the fashion industry, high-quality

After the bark has been boiled to a mush, it is pounded to further break down the fibers.

A sampling of the 2,000-plus papers produced for the Community Meal project.

The Ghana Paper Project produces materials for interior design, fashion, and packaging in addition to art and bookmaking.

paper is now being produced for artistic and functional purposes. Krataa Foundation papers are used in folding screens, lamps, and other objects for the high-end interiors market, as well as for gift wraps and bags for a broader market. One notable project has been a fine-press book, *Listen, Listen: Adadam Agofomma*, celebrating the musical legacy of Ghanaian musician Koo Nimo. Along with a specially produced musical CD, it includes hand-bound letterpress-printed pamphlets and a suite of intaglio and relief prints produced by Ghanaian artists Atta Kwami and Pamela Clarkson, all using locally produced handmade paper.

Currently, The Ghana Paper Project is establishing a self-sustaining papermaking enterprise that will employ a local workforce in the harvest, preparation, and production of high-quality handmade paper. For Hark, who continues to divide her time between the United States and Ghana, it all comes back to the paper. "Developing papers with beautiful surfaces is a great pleasure," she says. "It celebrates fine craft and satisfies my deep interest in process."

Learn more about Hark! Handmade Paper Studio, study opportunities, and the Ghana Paper Project at www.maryhark.com.

"Developing papers with beautiful surfaces is a great pleasure."

Aimee Lee Makes Hanji

Handmade paper, torn into strips and twisted, is knitted into pages for Lee's series of poetry books.

FOR AIMEE LEE, IT STARTED with books, making books, making artists' books. Books that combined writing, imagery, and storytelling. This was at Oberlin College in the late 1990s. But the paper! Who made the paper?

In graduate school at Columbia College Chicago, she learned to make her own paper in the classic European way, pulp on mould, and to bind her books according to European tradition. And this was good. But there was Korean paper, *hanji*, that spoke to her family origins, and no one in the United States was making it. Japanese and Chinese methods were being practiced, yes, but Korean ways didn't attract the same attention and respect. As was usually the case, Korea was "in the shadow" of these more culturally prominent nations.

So Lee went to Korea on a Fulbright Fellowship in 2008-2009 to learn all she could. "I milked the Fulbright for all it was worth," she says, "and why not?" She not only learned the history, the skills, the discipline, the craftsmanship, but she also

Traditional *hanji* paper comprises two thin layers.

documented everything. Her acclaimed book, *Hanji Unfurled: One Journey into Korean Papermaking*, was published a short three years later in 2012 by The Legacy Press. Yet another way to make a book.

She used her hanji to make books, as one would expect, but there was all this leftover scrap. Her mother grew up poor, her father was frugal, so in her background, even the scrap had value. Late in graduate school, she began to experiment with spinning the scrap into thread, first with her fingers, much later with a bobbin winder, and even later with a drop spindle. During her Fulbright year in Korea, she learned

Text in Lee's books is often suggestive, ephemeral.

another way of twisting and plying paper into cords, and then twining this cordage into splendid, sturdy baskets with classic or whimsical shapes, or both. Her series of woven ducks plays on a Korean wedding tradition but with an affectionate twist.

Korean paper, known as hanji, is made from the strong, lustrous fibers of the inner bark of the paper mulberry tree, but Lee uses many other plant sources: other types of paper mulberry (from Thailand, China, Japan, Korea, and Florida), milkweed, sometimes abaca or yucca, and more. A favorite is the long, strong fiber of milkweed stalks that she collects only after the monarch butterflies have left for their annual migration south. She also colors her paper with plant dyes.

KNITTED BOOKS

But let's circle back a bit. Before going to Korea, before learning hanji, Lee began making knitted books, that is, small, precious books with knitted pages. She used long strips of paper, sometimes spun in the

> "I would tell the mulberry to be the paper I wanted it to be... But that is going all backward. You must ask the mulberry what it wants to be."

Lee often chooses the complex and rhythmic Italian sestina poetry form for her books.

Japanese *shifu* way, sometimes barely twisted at all. Purling with loose tension was her technique of choice given the unforgiving, inelastic nature of the paper "yarn."

The pages are naturally ambiguous; the knitted structure is all holes and gaps. The technique informs the content: she makes books about a friendship breakup, about growing up between languages, between cultures. Pages fold back on each other or spill out of their bindings. Some have fragmentary ideas typed on paper and stitched to the pages; some have intricate poems in the spiraling, challenging Italian sestina format. They are perfect examples of meaning and form coming together.

WHAT NEXT?

For all its relative fragility, paper is hard work in the making. It is physically demanding, from harvesting and stripping the inner tree bark, to cooking it to neutralize acidic elements and balance the fiber's pH, to beating and agitating, to forming the sheets, to pressing, parting, and drying, to burnishing by hammering to smooth and compact the fibers. Each step requires meticulous, muscular attention. And the baskets demand great, punishing hand strength.

Lee considers that, given the physical demands of her craft, she has perhaps 20 more good years of active practice, so she spends more time teaching, more time designing and stitching paper garments and collages. She gives more thought to pacing herself and is actively thinking of her next book: about the makers of the hand tools and machines of the craft of papermaking.

In the end, she will listen to the materials to see where they take her, as she has always done. On a visit to Japan, an older papermaker said to her of his earlier years, "I would tell the mulberry to be the paper I wanted it to be... But that is going all backward. You must ask the mulberry what it wants to be."

To see more of Lee's work and the learning opportunities she offers, go to www.aimeelee.net.

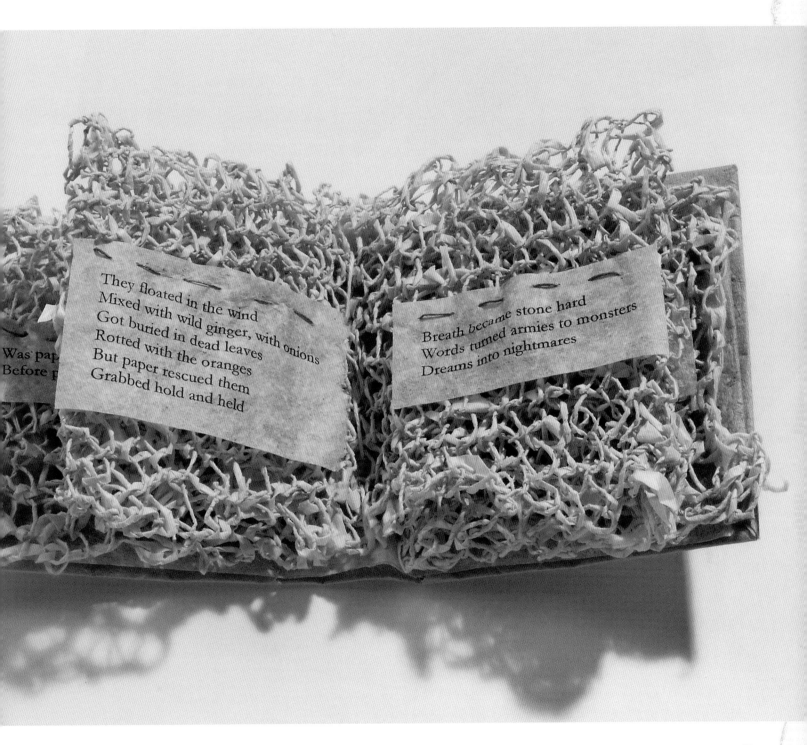

Sarah Swett and The Joy of Rubbish

Of course you can spin paper coffee filters. Even used ones. You can rinse them out, lay them flat to dry (no need to iron), scissor them into long, loopy slivers that want to be spun into a sturdy yarn of great character.

But would you?

Sarah Swett would. She operates at the intersection of thrift and imagination. Her coffee-filter yarn is just a beginning. It becomes weft for wee tapestries that cover tiny books, it becomes twining for emphatic baskets, it becomes a knitted dress. Why not? No limits.

Swett's weekly blog, A Field Guide to Needlework, documents her experiments with spinning, natural dyeing, knitwear design, life.
www.afieldguidetoneedlework.com

> Paper coffee filters come in many shapes and sizes, bleached or unbleached. Chemex filters (a sample of which follows) are 20 to 30 percent heavier than most other brands. Melittas might be made from bamboo pulp or softwood deciduous trees. Check the labels.

Today at my house

there is coffee filter yarn.

The sun is shining.

*And the narcissus—
almost blooming—*

are casting shadows on the wall.

A *flight* of cranes

JAPANESE LEGEND HAS IT that anyone who folds a thousand paper cranes, *senbazuru*, will be granted a wish by the crane god. Or perhaps in lieu of just one wish, happiness and good luck for life. Which would you choose?

> Paper cranes in Japan are typically folded from 3-inch squares of origami paper, although any other size is possible. Our cranes are folded from squares of Korean *hanji* paper, which has a lovely translucent quality. Ours came from Paper Connection International. You can find instructions for the 52 requisite steps to fold a crane on a number of internet sites.

Elegant Worm Spit

MICHAEL COOK

SILK IS AN AMAZING FIBER—strong, shiny, supple, and durable. Different kinds of silk have been raised and traded around the world for millennia, and silk has been used to make electrical insulation, to suture wounds, and to make a dazzling array of fabrics for applications from wedding gowns to parachutes. The six silk cocoons featured in these pages are from the most commonly exploited domestic and semidomestic silkworms: Bombyx, Tussah, Muga, Eri, Tasar, and Tensan. The cocoons are made by different species of silk moth caterpillars, also called silkworms. Bombyx are from family

Bombycidae, the silkworm moths; the others are from family *Saturniidae*, the giant silk moths.

The method for spinning cocoons is the same for all silk-producing caterpillars. The silk cocoon is formed by the caterpillar as a housing to protect it while it goes through the delicate and vulnerable process of changing into a moth. The silk comes from the caterpillar's silk glands—long narrow tubes full of a protein gel. This gel consists of two proteins: fibroin and sericin. Fibroin is the long, shiny fiber; sericin is a sticky, gum-like protein that binds the fibers of the cocoon together. The gel is extruded through two tiny openings in the head called spinnerets. The silk doesn't actually come out of the mouth, but the caterpillar uses some of its mouth parts, the mandibles, to handle the silk, resulting in people calling it "worm spit"—which is how I got the name for my website, www.wormspit.com.

There is a silk gland with a spinneret on each side of the caterpillar, and folded up double, the glands run the full length of the body. By the time a Bombyx caterpillar is ready to spin, it is roughly 75 percent silk inside; the caterpillar shrinks as it spins the cocoon, like a balloon letting out its air or a toothpaste tube being squeezed empty. The silk protein hardens on contact with the air, and the sericin on the strands glues them together.

The strand produced by the caterpillar is called a bave. The bave consists of two even smaller strands, called brins, one from each of the two silk glands. The typical bave for a Bombyx cocoon is about 20 microns across; the brins after degumming are closer to 7 microns. (A micron is about 1/25,000 of an inch.)

This is not a story of how to spin, but one of how to understand and appreciate your materials and the creatures that produce them. Follow along and be amazed.

Bombyx *(Bombyx mori)*.

BOMBYX

ORIGIN: China; now farmed across the globe

SCIENTIFIC NAME: *Bombyx mori*

COMMON NAMES: Bombyx silk, Mulberry silk, China silk

PREFERRED FOOD: Mulberry leaves (*Morus*, various species)

ALTERNATIVE FOOD: Paper mulberry (*Broussonetia papyrifera*), Osage orange (*Maclura pomifera*)

Bombyx, from the mulberry-eating silkworm *Bombyx mori*, is the most ubiquitous cocoon of them all. It is the fiber of legend, it is the livelihood of farmers across the globe, it is the silk of trade and commerce. A single grade-A1 hybrid Bombyx cocoon can contain more than 1,500 yards of a single, unbroken filament, laid down over the course of three days of patient work by the caterpillar. Silk thread is stronger, per weight, than steel wire, and it can be used for applications as diverse as clothing, embroidery, surgical sutures, and wire insulation.

Bombyx silk, also called mulberry silk, China silk, or pure silk, is reeled from cocoons in a process involving hot water; the strands are snagged from the end of each cocoon with a brush and then wound together to make filament, which is then doubled, twisted, and plied to create a wide range of yarns, from near-invisible organzine to drapey knitting yarns.

Legend has it that the Chinese empress Xi Ling Shi discovered the wonders of sericulture, the art and science of silk, about five thousand years ago when a cocoon fell into her imperial teacup. Pulling it out with chopsticks, she noticed strands coming off the cocoon—and thus discovered the first silk thread. There is archaeological evidence that silk was used even earlier; images of silkworms on pottery have been found in some ancient Chinese archaeological digs. Silk was a closely guarded state secret of the Chinese for centuries, but it eventually made its way to Japan and Korea, and then to other countries in Asia, Europe, and around the world. These days, China raises most of the bombyx silk on the market, but India also produces significant amounts, and other countries in southeast Asia, Africa, the Middle East, and parts of South America produce bombyx silk. Several efforts were made to raise silk in the United States, starting with the Colonies and extending through World War II, but they failed repeatedly, mostly because of the cost of labor.

Raising Bombyx silkworms is labor intensive. Silkworms are one of the few fully domesticated insects, and they require human care at every stage of their brief lives. They are reared in trays, mostly indoors but in some places in semi-open sheds. They must be fed by hand up to five times per day, and the farmers work constantly to keep them fed and clean. Freshly hatched baby caterpillars are fed finely chopped, tender leaves in tiny trays; by the time they are a month old, they are given piles of leaves or even whole young branches. Mulberry trees, trimmed to special bush shapes to produce the best and most nutritious tender leaves, are raised in rows in huge fields to feed the silkworms. Here in Texas, the mulberry has been used as a landscape tree and there are also "bird-planted" feral trees, so I mostly scavenge my mulberry leaves.

Bombyx has been in domestication for more than five thousand years. The original wild silkworm whose cocoon caught the empress's eye would have been *Bombyx mandarina*, the wild mulberry silk moth. These still exist, flitting around the woods in China and much of Asia. Their cocoons are fairly small and are tan or yellow (picking up the carotenoids and xanthophylls that give fall leaves their hues). Over the course of centuries, *Bombyx mori* developed just as dogs developed from wolves, through care and selection. The modern form of the moth is flightless and produces a massive amount of silk compared to its wild ancestors. None of them can eat, though; many people think that this is a by-product of domestication, but it is true of *all* of the silk moths that they are unable to feed on nectar in the imago, or adult, stage. The adults exist to mate and lay eggs, perpetuating the species. They live on stored fat and moisture until they run out of one or the other, usually after about a week.

Because of their long history of cultivation in nations around the world, silkworms have developed many races, or strains, each of

Bags of cut Bombyx cocoons are sold as a skin treatment product.

Legend has it that the Chinese empress Xi Ling Shi discovered the wonders of . . . the art and science of silk . . . when a cocoon fell into her imperial teacup.

which have different qualities. There aren't as many kinds of silkworms as there are breeds of dogs, but it's the same idea. Some are easy to rear in humid conditions due to disease resistance; others make massive amounts of pure white silk but can't handle cold temperatures, and so on. Strains that have been developed over centuries in specific areas are called landraces; they exist in basically any country where silk has been raised for a very long time. More modern agricultural races are sometimes identified by codes and numbers rather than names. I have raised several landraces of silkworms; they are surprisingly different from each other in every way, from their markings to their behavior. I've had caterpillars with skins ranging from creamy white to nearly black spin cocoons in every shade from pure white to chrome yellow and cotton-candy pink. I've had caterpillars go through their stages in anywhere from 17 to 34 days. Some wander all over, and others barely move aside from eating. In large-scale sericulture operations, hybrids are typically used. These are raised by specialists in rigorously maintained laboratory-farm facilities called grainages, and they are crossbred to create the best combination of silk quality, length of filament, percentage of perfect cocoons, vigor, disease resistance, and such. In many cases, the hybrids are complex, involving multigenerational crossbreeding to get the very best silk. A lot of this technology comes out of Japan and China. The Japanese were early leaders in using science to maximize silk yields, although nowadays, the Japanese produce very little of the world's silk.

Almost all of the silk produced in the world is bombyx silk. If a label just says "silk," it will be bombyx. This one moth accounts for something like 99.5 percent of the silk sold; all other species, including Tussah, Tasar, Eri, Muga, Tensan, and the various rare locally cultivated species, combine to make up the other one-half percent. The vast majority of the silk from Bombyx is reeled; the wastes from the reeling process, combined with wastes from cocoons that are cut open or hatched for breeding, are used to make spun silk. This includes silk at all of the intermediate stages (such as silk sliver or top) that is sold to handspinners or fed to the ring-spinning frames in large mills.

TUSSAH

ORIGIN: China; some from India

SCIENTIFIC NAME: *Antheraea pernyi*

COMMON NAMES: Tussah, Oak Tasar (in India)

PREFERRED FOOD: Oak leaves (*Quercus*, various species)

ALTERNATIVE FOOD: A variety of related tree leaves

The Tussah silkmoth, *Antheraea pernyi*, is raised primarily in China. India also raises some (called Oak Tasar), as well as a hybrid with *Antheraea roylei* called *Antheraea proylei*. These caterpillars do not take to indoor cultivation as do Bombyx; they have to be raised outdoors in fields. Some people have decided that this makes them "wild crafted," but that is not the case—they are guarded and managed as carefully as pastured sheep. They are reared on hillside plantations of specially bush-trimmed oak trees, and they are watched over to prevent predation by birds and other animals. Tussah cocoons are reeled like bombyx, using hot water, and are made into a variety of yarns and fabrics that rarely reach the Western market.

The filament that makes up the Tussah cocoon is coarser than that from Bombyx and flatter in cross-section, more like fettuccine than spaghetti. This gives Tussah a toothy hand and makes it more grippy to spin. As with all the reelable silks, the best-quality fiber is produced by reeling, and then the wastes from the reeling process plus cocoons that are damaged or unfit for reeling are degummed, carded, and combed to make fiber that is spun into a variety of yarns. The stuff that we can buy in the handspinning market in the West comes from the industrial supply process—it is designed and produced for the convenience of machines, but we have adapted it for use in handspinning.

I've raised Tussah and its American cousin, Polyphemus. I have to keep them carefully identified in marked bags, because the cocoons, and the resulting silk, are so similar. Polyphemus was investigated for the feasibility of commercial exploitation during the Colonial period, but it never really took off, largely because it was difficult to manage the caterpillars outdoors. I raise them in plastic shoe boxes. The main challenge is that while a shoe box can hold about 50 Bombyx caterpillars at their final full-grown larval stage, only 8 to 10 Polyphemus larvae can live in a shoe box. If they're crowded, they tend to get sick and fail to thrive.

Tussah (*Antheraea pernyi*).

Muga (*Antheraea assamensis*).

MUGA

ORIGIN: Assam, India

SCIENTIFIC NAME: *Antheraea assamensis*

COMMON NAMES: Muga, Munga, Moonga, the Gold of Assam

PREFERRED FOOD: Som (*Persea bombycina*), Soalu (*Litsea monopetala*), and Dighloti (*Litsea salicifolia*) leaves

ALTERNATIVE FOOD: A large number of related plants

Muga silk comes from the cocoon of the Assam silk moth, *Antheraea assamensis*. This silk has a distinctive, almost-metallic look; the filament often resembles fine brass wire. It is frequently referred to as the "Gold of Assam" for its golden color and for the value it holds both economically and culturally. Muga silk is given a place of special reverence in Assam and is used for many culturally significant garments, particularly bridal saris. It is used for rituals and ceremonies, sacred dance costumes, and garments for special events. As with Tussah and Tasar (see pages 32 and 38), Muga silkworms are raised outdoors on trees, frequently shepherded by young children who watch over them to keep the birds at bay. Tussah is reeled, often by hand in villages but increasingly using semiautomated reeling machines. On the other hand, muga reeling and sometimes tasar reeling involves something called false twist—this means rubbing the filament back and forth across a surface to agglutinate the fibers. There have been government efforts to remove "thigh-reeled" muga from production because it can cause skin issues when the silk is literally rolled against the thigh or sometimes the forearm. Unfortunately, as is so often the case with traditional textiles, the substitute version (reeled using a special "reeling pot" that looks like an upside-down bowl) doesn't yield the same quality of product as the original.

Muga is often woven "in the gum," without removing the sericin. (If the gum is removed, the silk becomes softer but loses its color and some of its sheen.) The stiffness from sericin creates body and crispness for many of the fabrics made from muga. Muga has received a geographical designation mark tying it to the state of Assam. As is the case for champagne, if it doesn't come from the designated region, it doesn't get the special name.

ERI

ORIGIN: India

SCIENTIFIC NAME: *Samia ricini*

COMMON NAMES: Eri, Endi, Errandi

PREFERRED FOOD: Castor (*Ricinis communis*) and tapioca (*Manihot esculenta*) leaves

ALTERNATIVE FOOD: Ligustrum, ailanthus, and many other tree leaves. In fact, this is the second-easiest silkworm to rear in captivity, although it can be challenging to find a source for the eggs.

Eri is another domesticated insect, although it does not require quite as much coddling as Bombyx. In fact, this is the second-easiest silkworm to rear in captivity, although it can be challenging to find a source for the eggs. Its history isn't as long, or in some parts, as clear. The DNA evidence shows that it is a polyhybrid of multiple *Samia* species including *Samia canningi* and *Samia cynthia*. At this point, they are distinct from any wild species, although they can be crossed back to some of the wild types. *Samia cynthia*, a relative to Eri, was introduced along with its food tree, *Ailanthus altissima*, into North America during the Colonial period in an attempt to provide an American wild silk industry; it became naturalized in the American northeast, although it is not common anymore.

Eri silkworms spin a discontinuous cocoon, meaning that the filament isn't laid down in one long, reelable length. Some sources I've read say that Eri is a "lazy spinner" because it doesn't work diligently like Bombyx but takes breaks. Because of this, reeled eri silk is not available, and it's all spun. In traditional culture, the cocoons are often degummed and spread into small cakes: the fiber is then pulled out and spun with a spindle. In commercial production, the cocoons are cleaned, carded, combed, cut to length, and made into sliver for machine spinning, just like any of the waste silk fibers. Eri silk has a matte, cotton-like hand in most fabrics, and it is considered a cheaper option than the fine, shiny bombyx or tasar silks.

Eri cocoons come in red and white. The red is typically a brick-like, brownish red, and the white is more like cream. These colors are in the sericin, the outer layer of the silk, and they are removed if the silk is softened by degumming.

> Several kinds of silk cocoons, both wild and cultivated, are available from Treenway Silks (www.treenwaysilks.com) as well as silk hankies or caps formed from stretched cocoons.

Red and white Eri (*Samia ricini*).

Tasar (*Antheraea mylitta*).

TASAR

ORIGIN: India

SCIENTIFIC NAME: *Antheraea mylitta, Antheraea paphia* (old name)

COMMON NAMES: Tasar, Tussar, Tropical Tussah, Tussah

PREFERRED FOOD: Arjun (*Terminalia arjuna*), Asan (*Terminalia tomentosa*), and Sal (*Shorea robusta*) leaves

ALTERNATIVE FOOD: Leaves from Indian jujube (*Ziziphus mauritiana*), axlewood (*Anogeissus latifolia*), jambul (*Syzygium cumini*), kumbhi (*Careya arborea*), anjan (*Hardwickia binata*), teak (*Tectona,* various species) and crape myrtle (*Lagerstroemia,* various species)

Tasar, eri, and muga are often referred to as the "vanya" silks in Indian literature. They're the silks of the forest, raised in tropical jungles and shrouded in mystery. Tasar caterpillars live most of their lives in trees and spin massive cocoons the size of hens' eggs with distinctive peduncles, or stalks. All of the *Antheraea* silks have some version of a peduncle; the caterpillar will spin a special little ribbon of silk to hold the cocoon onto the tree and prevent it from falling to the ground. With Tussah (and its American cousin, Polyphemus) this peduncle is a flat band of silk that holds a clump of leaves onto a branch, and often the best way to find cocoons in the wild is to look for clusters of leaves hanging on a bare tree. With Tasar, the peduncle and the outer layer of the cocoon are made from a cemented mixture of silk and tree bark; the caterpillar chews up the bark and mixes it into the silk as it spins, making these cocoons surprisingly hard to the touch. The peduncle looks as if it is made of wood—like a vine tendril—with a distinctive ring shape at the end where the caterpillar worked it around the branch. Tasar peduncles are considered a special grade of waste; they can be degummed and made into a variety of rough yarns. The cement layer has to be softened and removed before the cocoons can be reeled, typically using a harsh alkaline bath.

In different parts of tropical India, varieties of the Tasar caterpillar have been developed for varying silk applications—some silks are finer, others are paler, and so forth. These caterpillars are considered landraces and are distinctive to the regions where they're raised. They are fed a variety of trees to create specific textures and colors of silk.

Tasar silk, like muga and eri, is often used in specialty garments, and it is almost entirely consumed in India. Although the vanya silks have become more available in the Western market through global commerce, they still represent a very small niche in the silk marketplace.

> Some of the cocoons featured here and the rustic yarn spun from Tasar peduncles are available from www.habutextiles.com.

TENSAN

ORIGIN: Japan; some production in North Korea and China

SCIENTIFIC NAME: *Antheraea yamamai*

COMMON NAME: Tensan

PREFERRED FOOD: Kunugi oak leaves (*Quercus acutissima*)

ALTERNATIVE FOOD: Other oak leaves

Many think that muga is the most expensive commercial silk in the world, but tensan is much more dear. On the ground in Japan, my source tells me that Tensan cocoons go for about $3 apiece, and the textiles made from them are definitely luxury-priced goods. Production is very small, and it is consumed entirely within the country. Some Tensan is raised in North Korea and China to supply the Japanese market. It's beautiful stuff.

The spectacular green color is only present in the outer layer of the cocoon, and it's fugitive to heat. The cocoons are handled very carefully, reeled in tepid water, and moved to a different process once they lose their green shade. The inner cocoon, although much more silver than green, is brilliantly shiny and is used to make spun thread. When I raised Tensan, I found that the cocoons were much more of a tennis-ball yellow-green color and lacked the green hue I was hoping for. I suspect that this was due to a combination of the food species (I was using local red oak) and the mineral content of the soil.

To see the miracle of a Cecropia caterpillar metamorphosing to a moth, visit **https://www.thecaterpillarlab.org/pupation-video-resources**.

> Voltinism refers to the number of broods per year. Some species are univoltine, meaning that they will overwinter in one form or another, and each organism will live roughly a year between caterpillar, pupa, and moth stages. Bombyx and Tensan overwinter as eggs; the rest overwinter as pupae in their protective cocoons. Some of the tropical kinds, including Eri and the tropical Bombyx landraces, do not overwinter at all—they are multivoltine, or continuously brooded. This can be a problem if you're raising them in a climate where the trees drop their leaves—they will hatch whether or not there is food waiting for them.

Tensan (*Antheraea yamamai*).

The Handstitched World of Sarah K. Benning

BY ANNE MERROW

Picture a bright space with a chair ready for curling up with a book. The room is filled with luxurious foliage, not just one shade of green but a variety of leafy colors with textures that invite you to run your fingers across their surfaces. A cozy cabled sweater wards off the chill, and a vintage carpet covers the floorboards. It's the kind of room where you'd spend an afternoon in search of serenity and creativity.

Cozy Reader, original embroidery for *Washington Post* "Best Books of 2019."

Mini Potted Jungle 161, original embroidery measuring about 3" × 3".

SPACES LIKE THIS ARE a favorite subject of embroidery artist Sarah K. Benning. Not coincidentally, they also look a lot like a corner of her home studio, where she stitches one-of-a-kind pieces and creates designs to inspire other needleworkers.

When looking at Benning's artwork, it's difficult to keep your hands to yourself. The broad foliage of her plant images has the smooth, lightly cushioned surface of satin stitch, while the nubbly embroidered upholstery or the tiny spikes of cacti tempt you to pluck at them with a fingertip.

Benning turned to embroidery to find an outlet for expression without expectations, learning to stitch after years of intensely competitive art school. "I felt so completely burnt out that I didn't think I wanted to pursue any kind of artistic career," she says. "The gallery system felt very closed off and unwelcoming, and I turned to craft to sidestep the whole situation."

Working in embroidery places her at the intersection of art and craft, a space that many makers avoid. "I very much viewed embroidery as a step away from my fine art background. In fact, I specifically picked up a needle and thread and set about teaching myself embroidery because I was craving a creative pastime outside of the mainstream art world and free from the mostly self-imposed pressures of making Fine Art," Benning explains.

What she had viewed as turning away from art actually became the first step in finding her artistic voice. "Over the past seven years, the line between fine art and craft has dissolved for me," she remarks. "My embroidery is my art. It is my studio practice. It is my passion."

NEW PATHS

Stepping outside the traditional art world gave Benning the ability to reach new audiences and opportunities directly, finding buyers on Etsy and admirers on Instagram. Her work appeared before its largest viewership to date as the editorial illustration for the "Best Books of 2019" story in the *Washington Post*. The story's main pieces feature lush green plants and readers buried in books. She used the spur of a tight deadline to explore a new direction for her work: playing with negative space. Instead of covering the entire piece

"I primarily use satin stitch to create fields of solid color and sometimes add other stitched details to create additional texture or surface patterns. Then I outline each shape in black to further define each element in the composition. The whole process is very intuitive for me. I don't usually start out with a complete plan when it comes to color or particular textural elements, instead letting the piece develop more organically and just doing what feels right in the moment."

with tight, overlapping stitches, she filled certain areas while leaving some as plain cloth with only outlines.

In her self-directed studio work, she continues to play with using filled and empty areas of cloth in new pieces. "Art making is an ever-evolving and changing process," she says. "It is never static for me, and I'll never 'arrive' at an endpoint."

You can trace her development as an artist through her stitching motifs, stitching styles, and perspective. "My work has changed quite a lot over the past seven years," Benning points out. "I didn't find my way to houseplants as subject matter until maybe a year and a half into things, and it was another year before I started expanding that subject matter to include interiors and rugs, and even longer still until I added figures into the mix."

DRAWING WITH THREAD

Benning approaches her work as drawing with needle and thread. "Each piece begins either as a drawing made directly on the fabric (with pen or pencil) or as a digital drawing printed on stabilizer and applied to the fabric that way," she says. "Then the stitching process is more like coloring in the design."

Alien Scientist, original embroidery for *Washington Post* "Best Books of 2019."

Benning has begun working on a new large-scale original piece, outlining the printed figures in black before intricately stitching the plants.

THE ARTIST'S LIFE

Embroidery is not only Benning's primary mode of expression, it is also her family's business. Although her primary work is sketching and stitching original pieces, which she offers for sale through her online shop, she also makes some designs available as patterns and kits.

She began offering DIY options in response to customer demand, both by request and after she noticed her work being copied. "I actually release very few of my designs as kits or patterns," Benning says. She does offer embroidery transfers, a monthly pattern subscription, and complete kits (assembled in small batches by her husband and partner, Davey). Managing her original artwork and the demand for craft designs from their home studio poses its own challenges. "There is certainly an aspect of balance when exploring new ideas and creative expressions while also running a business that supports my family," she says, "but I try to follow my own instincts and intuitions about the work that I need to make rather than predict the market or let my community influence my work too much."

And that balance has allowed Sarah K. Benning to forge her own colorful, textural space as an artist—using needle and thread to find her voice, make her living, and share her vision.

You can see Benning's original artwork and purchase her kits at **www.sarahkbenning.com**.

Plant Queen,
11" × 11".

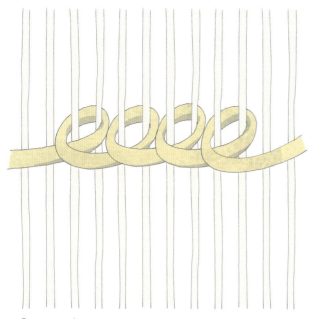
Open soumak.

Closed soumak.

Exploring Soumak

SAMPLES BY SARA LAMB

IT CAN BE AS SIMPLE AS THIS: Let's say you have a warp stretched on a simple frame. And instead of passing the weft over, under, over, under as you would for plain weave, you pass the weft over four, behind two, over four, behind two, and so on. You loop the weft around the warps rather than passing it straight across. That is soumak in its simplest form. But there is so much more.

This technique has been used for thousands of years to make sturdy rugs and bags, often beauti-

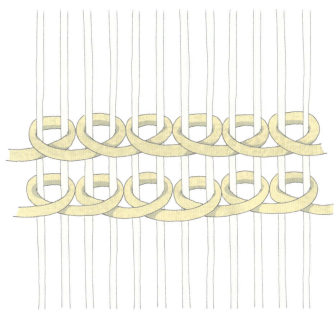

Open countered soumak, worked left to right and then right to left.

fully patterned, and to add pattern and texture to plain-weave fabrics. The earliest existing fragment of soumak dates to the seventh century BCE and was found in what is now Turkey. The technique is used to this day throughout Central Asia.

If you want to try it, you can use a basic frame, or a simple rigid-heddle loom, or a floor loom, or a tapestry loom—whatever will hold the warp taut. If you are going to weave a background fabric, as seen in these samples, you'll be glad if you have a way to automatically lift alternate warps instead of having to insert the plain-weave wefts by hand. The soumak rows, though, are always wrapped by hand.

It sounds simple, but one of the beauties of soumak is how endlessly variable it is. You can wrap in the over four, behind two sequence described earlier, or you can go over two, behind one for a tighter fabric. You can work right to left, then left to right for a herringbone effect. You can wrap multiple times around the same set of warps before moving on. You can take off on a diagonal to create a raised pattern on the plain-weave ground. You can alternate two colors to create a braided effect. You can use different weights and finishes of yarn, and you can devise unlimited polychrome designs, as you would see in tribal bags and rugs from centuries ago, or today.

Study these elegant samples woven by master weaver Sara Lamb. Match them to the technical illustrations to see how her effects were achieved. Then make soumak your own.

You can see in the following samples how simply varying the yarns can change the texture and surface reflectivity of the piece. Each yarn brings different elements to the surface of the fabric: some yarns show the patterns more distinctly, some less; some are fuzzy, some are smooth.

Sample 1

The top pattern band is worked in a hard-twist reeled silk. See how the twist in the yarn is emphasized as it passes back and forth? Does the back and forth looping motion actually add twist to the yarn? That would be worth observing.

The center pattern band is worked in a soft-twist 8/2 soft reeled silk. Loop definition is easy to see in this band.

The bottom pattern band is 20/2/5 spun silk. It has more plies but a very hard twist.

Sample 2

Like the previous sample, this one is worked in open countered soumak, but several yarns are used in the same row: some shiny, some matte. The selvedges are wrapped with extra weft, but they are still not as structurally sound as the closely wrapped center section.

Sample 3

Three-ply cotton forms the main area of this sample, and even though it is firmly spun, it has a nonreflective, matte finish that contrasts nicely with the reeled-silk center motifs.

Sample 4

The solid yellow band at the top of this sample is a cabled cotton yarn. Finer yarns in different hues are doubled or even tripled to match the weight of the yellow and used to create color blending. Patterning in soumak can be as bold or as subtle as you please.

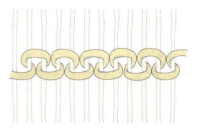

Alternating weft wrapping.

Diagonal weft wrapping.　　　　Vertical weft wrapping.

Sample 5

This sample uses the three wrapping techniques shown on this page. The diagonals came out too flat at the beginning. Using four passes of the foundation weft instead of two between each soumak row made the angles steeper. Reverting to two passes of foundation weft in the center section allows the wrapping to pack in tighter.

Sample 6

This sample uses several outlining wraps. On the left are two vertical outline wefts. On the right, two versions of diagonal wraps.

Soumak is a versatile textile structure; there is a wide variety of textures and patterning possible. It can be allover patterning, or used in small areas to accent or outline, in warp-faced weaves, or as a flat-weave area in a pile-weave structure. Soumak can be varied in several ways; by the number of ends wrapped, by the direction of wrapping, and by varying the size and colors of the wrapping yarns. It creates a sturdy textile that will be long lasting. While presenting a flat weave surface, there is really a whole lot going on inside the soumak textile that makes it a durable fabric for hard-use applications.

You can see more of Sara Lamb's weaving at her website, **www.saralamb.com**.

Resources

Collingwood, Peter. *The Techniques of Rug Weaving*. New York: Watson-Guptill, 1968.

Lamb, Sara. *Woven Treasures*. Loveland, Colorado: Interweave, 2009.

Mallett, Marla. *Woven Structures*. Atlanta: Christopher Publications, 1998.

Tanavoli, Parviz. *Shahsavan: Iranian Rugs and Textiles*. New York: Rizzoli, 1985.

Wilson, Jean. *Jean Wilson's Soumak Workbook*. Loveland, Colorado: Interweave, 1982.

Sample 7

Two-color wrapping opens up whole new worlds of possibility. The top and bottom borders look similar but have different wrapping sequences. The center gives a strong diagonal pattern.

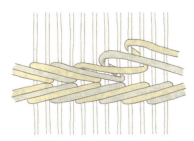

Two-color, two-strand weft wrapping variation.

Two-color, two-strand weft wrapping.

Two-color, two-strand weft wrapping variation.

Everything That Surrounds Us, 2019, magnolia leaves, cotton thread.

SUSANNA BAUER'S WORK COMES FROM THE intersection of two strong interests: art and nature. You can follow her "making" thread from early childhood, when knitting and crochet and creating things by hand were part of life, leading to a career as a model maker for film and advertising. The "nature" thread included working in a plant nursery in her younger days, working for a landscaping company, and later, pursuing a course of study in landscape architecture.

Susanna Bauer: A Thread, A Leaf

Core ll
(side view), 2015,
magnolia leaf, cotton thread.

Round, 2019, magnolia leaves, cotton thread.

"There is a fine balance in my work between fragility and strength: literally, when it comes to pulling a fine thread through a brittle leaf or thin, dry piece of wood, but also in a wider context—the tenderness and tension in human connections, the transient yet enduring beauty of nature that can be found in the smallest detail, the vulnerability and resilience that could be transferred to nature as a whole or through the stories of individual beings."

Realignment, 2019, magnolia leaf, cotton thread.

"I have always enjoyed making and creating; and knitting and crochet projects in the more conventional ways have been present throughout my life. I learned knitting, crochet, sewing, and embroidery on a basic level in primary school. My mother used to knit a lot and my grandmother was a seamstress, so I was surrounded by threads and material when I was young.

"My first works of this sort actually were a piece of branch collected in the woods and a smooth round stone. Spending time with these objects and taking them out of their usual cycle of life into a different context made me take in every little detail and look at what surrounds me in a different way. . . . Covering them in crochet and thereby . . . combining the craft technique with natural materials was my way of containing the experience that I associated with what I found."

Suspended (detail), 2018, magnolia leaf, cotton thread, wood.

Centered IX, 2019, plane tree leaves, cotton thread.

Restoration V,
2019, magnolia leaf,
cotton thread.

"My very first leaf piece just had a simple crochet edge. That was followed by a darned leaf, and I moved on to try out [my first three-dimensional piece], a leaf cube. These very early works were made in 2008, and many variations followed. Over the years, as my crochet skills developed, the patterns and constructions became more complex, but my main focus always lies on what each individual piece wants to express. The technicality of the making process for me is secondary.

"The fragility of life, relationships between us as human beings as well as with the environment, the precariousness of the natural world and its delicate balances, and my utmost admiration for nature's intricacies: all these are subjects that feed into my work and are universal to the human condition."

Navigation IX,
2019, magnolia leaf,
cotton thread.

Inner Circle, 2015, magnolia leaves, cotton thread.

"There is a lot of symbolism in the juxtaposition of a technique that relies on tension and a very fragile material—also looking closely at the fine details of leaves, the veins and shapes of each individual one, all different and unique, even coming from the same tree."

You can see more of Bauer's work on her website, **www.susannabauer.com**.

Together, 2019, magnolia leaves, cotton thread.

The Wonder of Lotus Fiber

WISDOM • PURITY • PEACE • SPIRITUALITY

THE VIRTUES ASCRIBED TO THE LOTUS plant (*Nelumbo nucifera*) in Asian history and lore are boundless. Every part of the plant has utility and virtue, whether medicinal, nutritional, spiritual, or all three. And it is beautiful, with pure, stately blossoms rising above large circular leaves, whole vast lakes of them. The flowers are harvested daily for religious and decorative uses. But overlooked for centuries, at least in the Western world, is the cloth woven from its fibers.

Besides all the aforementioned virtues, fabric woven from lotus fiber is wrinkle resistant, water-resistant, breathable, sturdy but sinuous, and comfortable in every way. It's said that in villages across India, Myanmar, Cambodia, and Thailand, the fiber has been harvested and crafted into special ritual cloth since ancient times.

And perhaps that's true. The practice had a "revival" in the early 1900s, a brief time when workshops in Japan and India began harvesting and processing and making this work known. It's extremely labor intensive, though, as you'll see, and these efforts languished until recently.

Lotus blossoms cover Tonlé Sap Lake near Siem Reap, Cambodia.

Up to 50 filaments can be drawn from each lotus stem. In a day's work, a single spinner can twist 250 meters of thread from 30 kilograms of stems.

FROM STEM TO CLOTH

We'll focus on Lake Kamping Poy near Battambat, Cambodia, where Samatoa Textiles has established a workshop to revive the craft. Around 15 hectares (37 acres) in area, the lake's surface is a vast field of lotus plants. Harvesters go out four times a day in narrow wooden boats to harvest the blossoms and slice off the stems for fiber. It takes 1 hectare, or 30 kilograms of stems, to supply a single spinner, who can produce 250 meters of thread per day.

Twenty-five thread makers are required to supply yarn for a single weaver.

"Spinning" isn't really an accurate description of how the thread is produced, though. Each stem is sliced through, and its 20 to 30 fine filaments are drawn out and hung to dry. They are then rolled by hand on a flat surface, with new fibers spliced in to create a long thread, suitable for warp or weft.

Twenty-five thread makers are required to supply yarn for a single weaver. The fabric is woven on a traditional Cambodian loom, 24 inches wide with two counterbalanced shafts and foot pedals. A typical warp is 100 yards long and takes about a month and a half to weave. A yard or so of fabric is estimated to require 32,000 lotus stems. You can see why the fabric is considered rare and precious.

A scarf woven of pure, undyed lotus fiber feels both earthy and silky, both warm and cool.

THE CLOTH ITSELF

Lotus fabric has been described as resembling a combination of silk and linen. In fact, it has a feel that's different from either. It is cool to the touch yet highly insulative, with a sleek hand and light weight that are at odds with its slightly rustic appearance. The individual fibers are similar in size to industrial microfibers, but instead of being solid extrusions, their structure is helical: a twisting flat ribbon of ladder-like spaces and cross-connectors (discernable only with the help of a scanning electron microscope). Its flat, twisting shape is similar to that of cotton.

The scarf at left is woven in plain weave at about 30 warp ends per inch. Where the threads hang loose in the fringe, they have tended to bloom and soften and feel like fine cashmere. They ignite readily but self-extinguish. This scarf's color is natural, but lotus fiber takes well to vegetal dyes, which have been used traditionally, and to some chemical dyes.

The Lotus Sutra, whose symbol is the lotus blossom, is an ancient document incorpo-

Lotus fabric takes natural dyes beautifully. These colors all come from local sources.

Lotus fabric is woven on traditional Cambodian looms in the Samatoa workshop.

Lotus fiber blends well with other natural fibers, as these samples show.

Grow your own

Lotus fiber for spinning isn't available from any commercial source, but you can grow your own. A backyard koi pond or other body of fresh water is ideal, but even a large pot on a sunny windowsill can work. The care and feeding of lotus plants is the same as for water lilies. Seeds and rhizomes and growing advice are available from many sites on the internet.

rating the final teachings of the Buddha. The sutra is considered, according to Western translators, "complete and sufficient for salvation." Like this sacred document, the lotus plant itself is complete and sufficient. Consider its nourishing rhizomes that thrive in the mud of shallow lakes; the stem that provides precious fibers; the pads and seeds, for which extravagant medicinal and nutritional claims are made; and the pristine and stately flowers, which have spiritual force across the globe. Use of its fiber for woven cloth is just one of the plant's many virtues.

Resources

Samatoa Lotus Textiles has a robust website with information and woven products for sale. Founder Awen Delavel conducts tours and product development workshops on-site and at the corporate office in Siem Reap, Cambodia. Find them online at **www.samatoa.lotus-flower-fabric.com**.

Patil, Kavita. "Lotus Fiber: A New Facet in Textile and Fashion." *International Journal of Humanities and Social Science Invention* 7, 12 (December 2018), 71–75.

Dyed yarns.

Michele Wipplinger:
A COLORFUL LIFE

BY KAREN SELK

Michele in northern Vietnam with a Hmong craftswoman in the mid-1990s.

EVERY NOW AND THEN, someone comes along who makes a big impact on the way we think about our earth. Michele Wipplinger was one of those people. She had a passion for color and textiles that propelled her life's journey. She was an author, educator, master dyer, traveler, photographer, designer, consultant, and owner of Earthues, a natural-dye company.

The textile community of weavers, spinners, quilters, knitters, dyers, stitchers, and felters was in the midst of a huge revival during the sixties, seventies, and eighties. We were exploring weave structures, spinning any fiber we could lay our hands on, making quilts that hung on the wall, felting funky hats, and experimenting with dyeing all of that cloth, yarn, and fiber with chemical and natural dyes. The few natural-dye books available instructed us on using flowers, roots, and bugs to color our cloth with the help of mordants. Most of those mordants were heavy metals that were bad for the environment and our health.

Michele was a pioneer, looking for another way to make natural dyes colorfast using nontoxic natural ingredients. The search for traditional methods used by other cultures took her on a lifelong quest through Europe; Southeast, South, and Central Asia; South America; and Africa.

HOW IT BEGAN

In 1978, as part of a two-year sabbatical from demanding careers, Michele and her husband, Andro, a chemical engineer, taking turns carrying their infant son, Solen, on their backs, hit the road to travel through Mexico and Central and South America in a van. Their initial quest was to find the dyers of coastal Oaxaca after seeing a documentary film back home in Seattle about their use of shellfish dyes.

"I felt as if I were standing in the midst of history," she said about her encounter with the local dyers who extracted the dye from caracol snails. "I realized this natural dyeing method had gone on

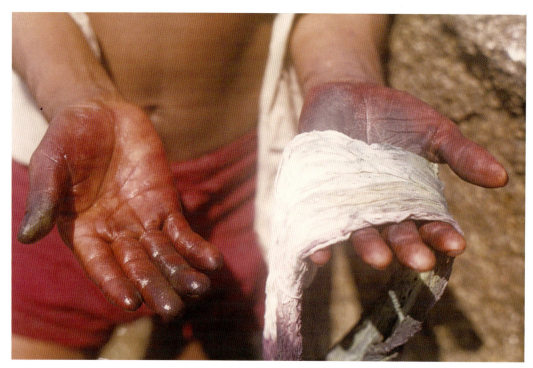

Sea snail dyeing on the Oaxaca coast.

unbroken since long before the Spanish conquistadors came. And it was still going on. I was in awe."

As she and her family continued their search for the sources of natural dyes, a second encounter months later in Bolivia sealed her future.

"We were standing on the Altiplano, the high desert area in the Andes, at maybe 12,000 feet. The sun was very different, very orange at that angle.

"That's when we saw this lone couple, campesinos they call them, a man and his wife walking with their llamas loaded with vegetables. He was playing his panpipe—a very high-pitched, eerie, soulful sound. It was an unforgettable moment.

Andro and I looked at each other. We felt as if we could be years in the past. Nothing had changed. Not a thing had changed. It was a very spiritual feeling. Seeing that man and his wife was almost like a message. It threw us back in history and forward to what we had to do."

MOVING ONWARD

Back in Seattle, with Andro settled in a career that could support the family, the quest continued. Michele and I were a natural team: I was in pursuit of silk, Michele explored natural dyes. We were seeking knowledge and understanding from those who had done this work for generations. We began our travels to far-flung parts of the world in the mid-1980s before the invention of the

> *"I felt as if I were standing in the midst of history. I realized this natural dyeing method had gone on unbroken since long before the Spanish conquistadors came. And it was still going on. I was in awe."*

internet. It was an adventure! Michele traveled with a camera, a journal, an open heart, a sense of wonder, and good humor. These crucial ingredients help any cultural and language differences melt into compassion.

We traveled via trains, planes, buses, cars, scooters, bicycles, ferries, rickshaws, and three-wheeled tuk-tuks. It takes many expeditions at various times of the year to villages of different tribes to acquire a picture of the whole process of working with a particular natural dye. It often takes numerous translations from village dialect to the broader spoken language to English. Sometimes the information did not line up, so we'd try again. Precision is important in understanding dye chemistry.

There were adventures both good and scary: 3 a.m., a train rushing through the room—no, a 6.2 earthquake 200 miles away! Maharaja Palace Hotel—half asleep, creepy crawly, turn the light on—bedbugs all over! An audience with the Dalai Lama in his Dharamshala home! Crossing the Mekong on a ferry run by a motorcycle engine, steered with a stick! Cuddling a baby tiger in Laos whose mommy had been poached! Wrong train—go up the stairs, over the footbridge to the trains going in the opposite direction—hurry, the train is boarding!

Amidst our adventures in reaching far-flung villages, it was the heart and soul of resourceful artisans using what was available in their region that brought awe, wonder, and respect: block printing mud onto cloth to act as a resist before dipping it into an indigo vat dug deep into the earth; cow dung used to bleach cotton; a bamboo reed wrapped with cotton cloth and tightly bound with string to become a pen for painting intricate designs on silk and cotton cloth using age-old natural-dye recipes; men singing the color sequence for knotting a silk carpet—no graph paper; strips of bicycle inner tube used to wrap weft threads as a resist for ikat dyeing and weaving; fluorescent green dye applied to cloth with a chicken feather, pounded on a rock and waved over a smoky fire to turn it a shiny bronze; indigo-dyed cotton applied with pig's blood and soy milk, pounded to create a burnt umber color; Tasar cocoons reeled by twisting the silk on women's thighs; hundreds of tiny 2-inch shuttles used to weave tapestry yardage.

These encounters created a bond with sisters and brothers in color and cloth. These artisans were proud, patient, kind, and caring, and eager to share their knowledge and secrets.

Lucky Strikes and Jack Daniel's, Burma, 1986

Traveling in Burma (now Myanmar) was only for the hardy and adventuresome in 1986. The Burmese people are gentle, easy souls, but the government-controlled Tourism Burma was right out of 1984. While we were in Thailand, other travelers had informed us we needed to prepare for Burmese customs and immigration, so we each bought a carton of Lucky Strike cigarettes and a bottle of Jack Daniel's whiskey. These were strategically placed on top of everything else in our suitcases. Our arrival seemed out of a Humphrey Bogart movie. The terminal in Rangoon remained from British colonial occupation: crumbling, with peeling white pillars, dirty palm ceiling fans, and open walls with a hot breeze flowing through, but holding evidence of better times. We queued up in the oppressive heat for hours while the officious customs agents inspected and closed each bag—minus the Lucky Strikes and Jack Daniel's.

By the time we legally changed a $50 bill into Burmese kyat, it was dark outside. It was all so surreal: the heat, the overbearing officers, the decaying grandeur, the unfamiliar smells, the dark, and the random lights that shone like purple strobes along the side of the road, attracting large grasshopper-like bugs. People of all ages gathered under the lights, grabbing the insects to take home for dinner. As we drove through the dark of Rangoon, lit only by candles on the vendors' carts, we had no sense that the streets radiated out like spokes from the Shwedagon Pagoda at the center of the city. It all seemed so shadowy, and we could not wait to reach our accommodation, the Garden Guesthouse. But even before we were shown to our room, we knew this was going to be one of the longest nights of our lives.

We settled in our "dorm" room, which had a cement floor and two small, hard beds shrouded in holey mosquito nets that were repaired with other travelers' Band-Aids. We hoped a shower would make us feel better equipped to make it through this night. I stepped into the dim, gang-style shower first and slid all the way to the other end on the slimy floor. Grossed out, but already in, I rinsed off in the cold water while Michele waited in case I slipped and fell. We went out into the night foraging for water

Michele with a village artisan in Rajasthan, India, in 1992.

and, we hoped, some familiar food. People huddled around candlelit carts smoking hand-rolled cigarettes and speaking only Burmese. We felt shy and vulnerable staring into the carts looking for water and food. We roamed aimlessly and lost track of which spoke we had come from. With panic in our hearts and stomachs, we made a few passes around the huge pagoda until we finally saw the sign for the Garden Guesthouse. We returned with watermelon, peanuts, and water in glass bottles with metal caps, like old-style Coca-Cola bottles. I opened the first bottle with my Swiss Army knife and passed it to Michele. Before I got the second bottle cap off, Michele cried, "I don't want to die in the Garden Guesthouse." The water smelled awful and tasted even worse. It was a long and very bizarre day. We lay down on the gray, dirty sheets fully dressed, each with our own somber thoughts and waited for the first light at 6 a.m. We were two naive, middle-class, white women who plucked up and gathered our wits on this new day.

We quickly found the best way to deal with Tourism Burma, located the most agreeable food for our palates and stomachs along with better water and accommodation, and learned how to deal on the black market in the backseat of a taxi to change money for a rate twice what the bank was paying. When all was sorted, we went in search of natural dyes and Burmese silk.

A Sandy Shower, India, 1990

Michele started making distressing sounds from the shower in our Delhi hotel. She couldn't see

Indigo dyer, India.

These encounters created a bond with sisters and brothers in color and cloth.

the long thread   79

Indigo dyer, Laos.

us in. He proudly flushed the toilet and walked out of the room. We held it together until he closed the door and then rolled on the bed in fits of laughter as the sand continued to drip out of the showerhead.

Rice Wine First, Laos, 2000

White cotton strings plucked from a central flower arrangement are tied around our wrists with whispers of good luck, happy travels, and finding a good man as part of a *baci* (calling of the soul) ceremony. The spiritual ceremony is presided over by an elder who has been a Buddhist monk at some time. Everyone at the ceremony receives many string bracelets and ties them on others, passing along good wishes. The baci is in our honor to welcome and wish good travels through their country. The reverent part of the ceremony takes place before noon, and then the party begins with lots of food and a communal 2-gallon clay jug filled with rice wine and containing two long bamboo straws. No one should drink alone. In fact, the guests of honor are called to sip the harsh drink over and over amidst the dancing and eating. We stagger out into the heat of the day. People giggle as they help the tipsy foreigners from the dock down into a small wooden boat. The weaving village is on the other side of the Mekong River.

WHAT CAME NEXT

I share these memories because they seem to stand in such contrast to the Michele that came later— the Michele who was a board member for the Color Marketing Group, who helped companies and organizations such as Aveda, Origins, Esprit, Martha

much without her glasses and called me to come in and tell her what was happening. Outside, men were digging in the garden. Sand was spurting out of the showerhead. Michele grabbed a robe, while I scurried downstairs to inform someone of the problem. Moments later, a knock at the door announced a man carrying a black doctor's bag with a plunger tucked under the handles. We led him into the bathroom and he closed the door. We sat on the bed. Twenty minutes later, we heard the toilet flush. He opened the door, beaming, and beckoned

Stewart Living, Terre Verde, L.L. Bean, and The Nature Conservancy develop products that could bring awareness of the value of natural colors to a larger world. Her vast knowledge and sense of color was sought by government and nongovernment agencies for the development of naturally dyed products throughout the world. She worked with Organization for American States, Aid to Artisans, VVF in Turkey, USAID, and UNESCO to help develop repeatable, sustainable, environmentally safe methods for creating beautiful colors for cottage industries, textile cooperatives, and small companies. By 1995, the L.L. Bean fall catalog had natural-dyed sweaters. And that year, she won the United Nations' Fashion Industry and the

Consulting with women in Laos on their color palette.

Environment Award for environmental stewardship and the development of an eco-friendly natural-dye process for the American textile industry.

The Michele of rickshaws and bedbugs may seem a far cry from the Michele of business suits and New York boardrooms, but her life was a continuous thread. It was spun from a passion for infusing the world with natural color, and thus making the world a better place. She has left us with an example of an active, purposeful life, full of curiosity, creativity, warmth, and joy.

Andro continues Michele's legacy through Earthues, a business working in partnership with artisans to fulfill their dreams. Visit it online at **www.earthues.com**.

Michele with an indigo dyer, India, 2006.

the long thread **81**

Indigo

i. PANGAEA

The ice recedes. New hunting grounds appear.
Your clan is creeping north from the savannahs.

It's cold. You make up ways to wrap the babies,
Your bodies, out of what you know, or you can find.

What you wear is white or brown or gray.
The world is green and blue and red and gold.

This bruised leaf oozes blue, the tuft of wool
pulled from a bush drinks the color in.

You break another leaf and rub your fingers.
What would you do to go dressed as sky?

ii. SCOTLAND

Your blades bounce off their armor. They are trained
in invasion. You just want your croft

clean of their footprints, so you can go back
To squabbling with your neighbors.

They're from far away. Stop. Turn that around.
They're far from home. Infiltrate their fears.

Paint your faces with the blood of plants.
Be the nightmare of a homesick man.

Their emperor sends word. They build a wall
across the country just to keep you home.

iii. GHANA

It is magic. When you lift the fabric
from the pot it is pale yellow-green;

becomes blue only at the kiss of air,
the opposite of blood. There are secrets.

It must be kept warm, not too bland or acid;
feed it a banana or a lime.

The dyer's tongue turns blue.
It must be tended and it can go bad.

When something goes wrong there is always blame:
men may not come near the pot, nor women

who are fertile and might drain its power.
The pot is living. This is a craft for crones.

Four different plants dispersed around the world
yield the chemical that makes this blue.

Spies and sailors, treaties and piracy
will jostle for it. It will bring in gold,

it will require whips and slavery.
What would you do to go dressed in sky?

~ SUSAN BLACKWELL RAMSEY, 2010

Who Writes This Stuff, Anyway?

Born in Germany, **SUSANNA BAUER** studied landscape architecture in Munich and art at the Camberwell College of Arts in London. She lives in southwest Cornwall with artist Paul Fry and their son, whom she homeschooled throughout the recent medical crisis.

MICHAEL COOK lives in Dallas, Texas, with his husband, Chris; his day job is Assistant Director of the Sammons Center for the Arts. His specialization in silk started in about 2001, when he found eggs on offer on a website. "It perfectly combined my 'Wow, I can make this awesome thing!' interest with my 'Lookit this COOL BUG!' interest." He's raised about a dozen different species and may have as many as a thousand tiny livestock in his upstairs studio room, munching on mulberry and other leaves.

ANNE MERROW is a knitter, spinner, editor, and cofounder of Long Thread Media. She lives and works in northern Colorado in a house full of yarn and fiber, to the delight of her cats and the despair of her spouse. The fleece in her photo is a Corriedale cross, one of about seven that she will admit to in her current stash.

SARAH SWETT lives in Moscow, Idaho, and devotes her days to handspun yarn: to making the yarn; to making things with the yarn; to drawing herself making things with the yarn; to writing about the drawings, the things, and the yarn; to running barefoot in the mud. Her self-portrait here was sketched on a coffee filter.

SUSAN BLACKWELL RAMSEY has taught ninth-grade English, first-year Spanish, the MFA workshop in Poetry at the University of Notre Dame, and, at the Kalamazoo Institute of Arts, creative writing, knitting, and spinning. Her book *A Mind Like This* (University of Nebraska Press) won the Prairie Schooner Poetry Book Prize. She lives in Kalamazoo, which does exist.

Textile artist **KAREN SELK** lives on an island in the Salish Sea off the coast of British Columbia. Silk has provided the thread that binds together travel, research, writing, artwork, educating, and managing a successful silk business. The serenity and beauty of island life inspire many hours in the studio creating art and writing. Growing the majority of their own organic food with husband, Terry, sleeping outside, yoga, friends, and family provide a balance.

Besides sitting in her son's firetruck, **SARA LAMB** thinks there is nothing more fun than weaving. "Well, maybe spinning. Wait! Dyeing is the most fun! Hmmmmm . . ." She is not a neat creator, and apparently thrives in the chaos. Every now and then, she cleans up, packs up, and goes out to conferences and workshops to meet up with old friends and make new ones, only to come home and find peace and joy, full of memories, reflections, and ideas. She would not be who she is without the everyday making of textiles and is grateful for having wandered into a weaving class, some 40-odd years ago.

CREDITS

COVER: Wild Tasar silk cocoons. Photo by Mary Staley Pridgen.

PAGE 2: Photo by Mary Staley Pridgen.

PAGE 3: Photo courtesy of Susanna Bauer. Photos by www.art-photographers.co.uk.

PAGES 4-5: Photos by Matt Graves.

PAGE 5: William Stafford, excerpt from "The Way It Is" from *Ask Me: 100 Essential Poems.* Copyright © 1977, 2014 by William Stafford and the Estate of William Stafford. Used with the permission of The Permissions Company, LLC on behalf of Kim Stafford and Graywolf Press, Minneapolis, Minnesota, www.graywolfpress.org.

PAGES 6-11: Photos courtesy of Hark! Handmade Paper.

PAGES 12-17: Photos courtesy of Aimee Lee.

PAGES 18-23: Photos by Sarah Swett.

PAGES 24-25: Photos by Matt Graves. Cranes by Ian Brock.

PAGES 26-41: Photos by Mary Staley Pridgen.

PAGES 42-49: Photos copyright Sarah K. Benning.

PAGES 50-55: Photos by Matt Graves. Illustrations by Ann Sabin Swanson.

PAGES 56-65: Photos courtesy of Susanna Bauer. Photos by www.art-photographers.co.uk.

PAGE 66: Photo by Joe Coca.

PAGES 68-69 AND 71-73: Photos courtesy of Samatoa Textiles.

PAGE 70: Photo by Matt Graves.

PAGES 74-81: Photos courtesy of Andro Wipplinger and Karen Selk.

PAGES 82-83: Poem and block print by Susan Blackwell Ramsey, from *Indigo*, Kalamazoo Book Arts Center, 2010.

thrumsbooks.com

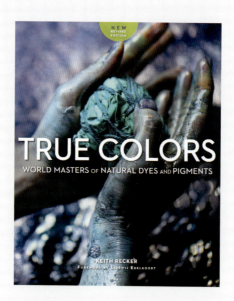

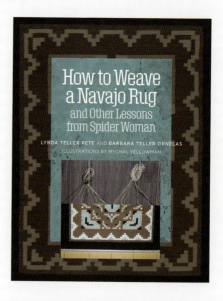

True Colors: World Masters of Natural Dyes and Pigments

REVISED EDITION WITH NEW CONTENT
Keith Recker

True Colors is about artists who create color from natural materials and about the historical importance and environmental sustainability of this practice. Deep conversations with 28 artisans from every part of the globe reveal their wisdom, traditions, and know-how—and suggest that we ignore what they know at our peril. Traditional approaches to making color offer sustainable options to a fashion system badly in need of them and memorable cultural narratives to a world hungry for beauty and spirituality.

Trade Paperback • $36.95 • 252 pages
ISBN: 978-1-7332003-8-7
Cultural Studies/Fashion
eBook formats available

How to Weave a Navajo Rug and Other Lessons from Spider Woman

Lynda Teller Ornelas and Barbara Teller Ornelas; Illustrations by Mychal Yellowman

How to Weave a Navajo Rug has detailed how-to instructions, meticulously illustrated by a Navajo artist, from warping the loom to important finishing touches. For the first time, master Navajo weavers themselves share the deep, inside story of how these textiles are created, and how their creation resonates in Navajo culture. This book is the only how-to book on Navajo weaving told by Navajo weavers.

Hardbound • $29.95 • 160 pages
ISBN: 978-1-7344217-0-5
eBook formats available
Cultural Studies/Craft

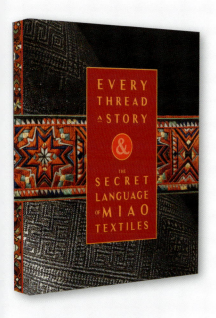

Every Thread a Story: Traditional Chinese Artisans of Guizhou Province *and* The Secret Language of Miao Embroidery
BOXED SET

Karen Brock, Linda Ligon, Wang Jun

US price: $49.95 • ISBN: 978-1-7332003-9-4
eBook formats available • Asian Studies/Cultural Studies/Textile & Costume Design

Every Thread a Story is a tribute to ethnic minority artisans of China's Guizhou Province. It is also a tribute to the heritage craft traditions and techniques passed down through the generations of their families. The book introduces more than a dozen contemporary artists from four ethnic groups working in the techniques of their ancestors, including indigo dyers, embroiderers of varying techniques, weavers, a metalsmith, and a paper maker. A wide-ranging look to the future questions the effects of tourism and modern development on the craft and culture of southeast Guizhou Province.

160 pages, 200 color photos

The Secret Language of Miao Embroidery presents, for the first-time, expert interpretations of the Miao symbols and motifs embellished on traditional clothing of the Miao peoples of China. Using examples from pieces in a museum's collection, the author provides clear descriptions and stories for the symbols and motifs found in highly collectible Miao textiles, focusing on southeast Guizhou Province. Detailed color photographs accompany each motif.

64 pages

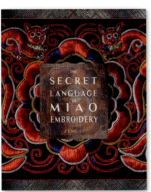

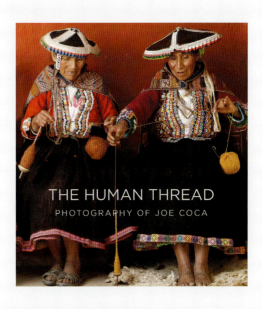

The Human Thread: Photography of Joe Coca
Joe Coca

The Human Thread is a celebration of outstanding photography. Over 100 images represent photographer Joe Coca's remarkable work, spanning forty years and five continents. Through evocative images and companion personal stories, he guides us on a global journey, weaving together place, people, craft, and story with the human thread that connects us all. Each section of the book features an array of exceptional photographs that shows a region's people as well as surprising glimpses of culture and environment.

Hardcover • $36.95
ISBN: 978-1-7335108-6-8 • 188 pages
eBook formats available
Photography/Cultural Studies

Access the education you've trusted for 40 years and the inspiration that keeps you creating now.

Get every issue of *Handwoven*, *Spin Off*, and *PieceWork*, as well as 100+ crafting videos for as little as $10 per month.

 follow the long thread

Visit **longthreadmedia.com** to subscribe today.